D0734308

The Oklahoma City Bombing

Titles in the *American Disasters* series:

The Exxon Valdez
Tragic Oil Spill
ISBN 0-7660-1058-9

Hurricane Andrew
Nature's Rage
ISBN 0-7660-1057-0

The Oklahoma City Bombing
Terror in the Heartland
ISBN 0-7660-1061-9

Plains Outbreak Tornadoes
Killer Twisters
ISBN 0-7660-1059-7

San Francisco Earthquake, 1989
Death and Destruction
ISBN 0-7660-1060-0

The World Trade Center Bombing
Terror in the Towers
ISBN 0-7660-1056-2

The Oklahoma City Bombing

Terror in the Heartland

Victoria Sherrow

Enslow Publishers, Inc.

40 Industrial Road	PO Box 38
Box 398	Aldershot
Berkeley Heights, NJ 07922	Hants GU12 6BP
USA	UK

http://www.enslow.com

Copyright © 1998 by Enslow Publishers, Inc.

Library of Congress Cataloging-in-Publication Data

Sherrow, Victoria.
    The Oklahoma City bombing: terror in the heartland / Victoria Sherrow.
        p. cm. — (American disasters)
    Includes bibliographical references and index.
    Summary: Details the events surrounding the 1995 terrorist bombing
of the federal building in Oklahoma City, as well as the investigation and
trial of those responsible for the blast.
    ISBN 0-7660-1061-9
    1. Oklahoma City Federal Building Bombing, Oklahoma City, Okla.,
1995—Juvenile literature. 2. Terrorism—Oklahoma—Oklahoma City—
Juvenile literature. 3. Bombing investigation—Oklahoma—Oklahoma City
—Juvenile literature. [1. Oklahoma City Federal Building Bombing,
Oklahoma City, Okla., 1995. 2. Terrorism. 3. Bombing investigation.]
    I. Title II. Series
    HV6432.S53   1998
    364.16—dc21   97-45750
                                                    CIP
                                                        AC

Printed in the United States of America

10 9 8 7 6 5 4

To Our Readers:
We have done our best to make sure all Internet addresses in this book were active and
appropriate when we went to press. However, the author and the publisher have no
control over and assume no liability for the material available on those Internet sites
or on other Web sites they may link to. Any comments or suggestions can be sent by
e-mail to comments@enslow.com or to the address on the back cover.

Photo Credits: AP/Wide World Photos, pp. 1, 6, 9, 13, 15, 18, 20, 22, 23, 24,
27, 28, 29, 33, 34, 35, 37, 39, 41.

Cover Photo: AP/Wide World Photos

Contents

CHAPTER 1

"This Isn't Supposed to Happen"

It was unforgettable—the booming noise that pierced the air in Oklahoma City on the morning of April 19, 1995. A ball of flame rose toward the sky. Within seconds, the front of the nine-story Alfred P. Murrah Federal Building had crumbled to the ground. A quiet spring day had become a living nightmare.

The bomb that devastated this building resounded for miles around. People within thirty miles of the city heard the noise and felt a tremor. Melva Noakes was working at a day care center in Choctaw, twenty miles from Oklahoma City. She remembered, "We went outside and saw a jet and thought [the explosion] must have been a sonic boom."[1] Some people thought the noise was thunder. They saw lights flash in the sky and wondered why lightning had struck on a clear day.

What had struck was a van loaded with four thousand eight hundred pounds of explosives. In that instant, 168 lives were cut short. Thousands of other people were left injured or grieving.

Some people inside the federal building survived the initial blast. One of them was Michael Reyes. His office was on the seventh floor. Reyes recalls what happened that Wednesday morning:

> I was sitting at my desk, and I had just gotten off the phone and then the power went off. And that was a weird sensation because the power had never gone off. And then I started hearing this rumbling, and I guess I thought it was an earthquake. I thought, 'I need to get under my desk' and then I looked at my desk. it was just shaking violently like it was going to break apart.[2]

Michael Reyes crouched under his desk. Then, suddenly, the floor gave way. He said, "I started to fall—but I was in a dive. And I thought, 'I'm just going to fall down seven floors and that's going to be it—it's just going to be over."[3]

On the third floor, staff members of the federal credit union office were meeting. They were seated around the desk of director Florence Rogers. As the bomb exploded, Rogers saw eight of her fellow employees plunge through the floor and into the ground.

Scientists would later explain that when the bomb went off, super-hot gas had streaked through the building at a speed of 8,000 feet per second. "Those standing out front were slammed with a force equal to 37 tons. One man, they said, who was taking a cigarette break outdoors, was vaporized into the wall."[4]

An instant later, the gas evaporated. A fierce vacuum formed. "Oxygen was sucked out of the air. The ground shook as if it were being tossed by a full-scale earthquake."[5]

This mighty explosion tore apart the federal building and sent glass and concrete flying onto the streets. Scattered in the dust and debris were children's toys. It was a dreadful reminder that a day care center had been operating inside the building. That morning, parents had arrived with their children as usual. Among them were A.C. Cooper and his wife, Dana, the director of the center. A.C. had dropped off Dana and their two-year-old son,

In the days after the bombing, anxiety would turn to horror and grief, as many learned that loved ones had died in the blast.

Anthony Christopher, then kissed them good-bye. It was the last time he would see them alive.

After the explosion, people from around Oklahoma City rushed to the bomb site to help. Black smoke swirled around them. Cars had been blown to pieces and parking meters were knocked down. Glass and concrete lay strewn along the sidewalks.

Among those who hurried to the site was Dolores Watson. Her grandson, P.J. Allen, had been in the day care center. Watson later said, "When I looked at that building, I didn't—I couldn't imagine anyone coming out alive out of that building."[6]

As they arrived, police and firefighters were visibly upset. Assistant Fire Chief Jon Hansen said, "This isn't supposed to happen in the heartland."[7]

CHAPTER 2

Hours of Agony

As rescue teams arrived, stunned survivors were emerging from the ruins of the bombed building. They were terribly wounded and burned. Others had no shoes, and their clothing hung in shreds. Some people had lost an eye, an arm, a leg, or fingers.

From the rubble, police and firefighters heard children crying. They hurried toward the sounds to find survivors. Police sergeant John Avera recalled, "We started moving bricks and rocks and we found two babies."[1] Medics gently wrapped the severely burned, barely living infants in white gauze.

In the face of this disaster, people came to help. There were medical and nursing students, off-duty police officers, clergy, engineers, and others. One hundred physicians from Oklahoma City had gone to a medical conference in Houston. When they heard about the bombing, they flew back home.

Stephen Pruitt was one of the injured. He was thrown

against a brick wall so hard that he had brick prints on his skin. His nose was broken and his eye was severely injured. Luckily, his injuries were less severe than those of some others.

Michael Reyes had fallen down four stories to the third floor. He was still conscious but badly cut and bruised. People who worked on that floor lowered him to ground level. From there, medics placed him on a stretcher.

Reyes asked about his father, who worked in another part of the building. Nobody could find him. In ten days, the family would find out that Michael's father had died. His office was in the worst-hit part of the building.

People outside the federal building also suffered severe injuries. Candy Avey had parked her car and was entering the building when the bomb went off. She says, "I was blown back, wrapped around the meter, and my face hit the car."[2] Avey suffered a broken arm and jaw. She described another victim who was entering the building: "His arm was blown off. But he was in such shock that he didn't even notice it. He just kept on going, attempting to help others around him."[3]

Flying glass caused many injuries, including punctured lungs. Nurse Shirley Moser said, "When you see what it does, you can't believe it. It's as though you filled a shotgun shell with slivers of glass and shot it at someone."[4]

Polly Nichols worked across the street at the *Journal Record* Building. Flying glass hit her in the throat and severely cut two major blood vessels. Nichols stumbled down a flight of stairs and collapsed. A co-worker carried her outside where a doctor got her into an ambulance. She later told reporter Wade Goodwyn, "I came within 10 minutes of dying."[5]

Dan Webber worked in an office in the courthouse down the street from the federal building. The force of the explosion threw him across the room. But Webber was much more upset by the fact that his three-year-old son, Joseph, was at the day care center. He raced down the

*R*escue workers from many different states and groups (as shown by the different flags) worked tirelessly to find survivors among the rubble.

street to his wife's office. Together, they ran to the bomb site and searched frantically for their son.

Twenty minutes later, a policeman walked by with Joseph in his arms. He was cut and bleeding, with a broken arm and ruptured eardrums. But the Webbers were overjoyed to find their child alive.

Dolores Watson's grandson P.J. was also found alive. He suffered burns and a fracture.

Two of the most distraught people at the bomb site were Jim Denny, a fifty-year-old toolmaker, and his wife, Claudia. Their two children, two-year-old Rebecca and three-year-old Brandon, were at the day care center. Denny was stunned when he saw the smoking ruins of the federal building. He later said, "I thought a nine-story building had disappeared."[6]

The Dennys rushed to a Red Cross center to wait for news of their children. A local news station reported that an unidentified little girl with long, red hair was in surgery at Southwest Medical Center. It was Rebecca Denny. She had serious cuts and burns, but doctors said she would eventually recover.

Where was Brandon? Hours later, the Dennys heard that a boy with reddish-blond hair was at Presbyterian Hospital. Inside the former day care center, Brandon was found covered in the dust and debris. His rescuer recalled, "I cradled [him] in my arms and noticed that he had a head injury and appeared to have a brick sticking out of his forehead. The boy was holding a little green block."[7]

Flying debris had torn a hole in Brandon's skull. He

*B*randon Denny (with his father) suffered severe injuries as a result of the bombing.

would remain in critical condition for several days. But his parents felt they had experienced two miracles that day.

For other parents, there were no miracles. Only six of the children in the day care center survived. Rescue workers found the body of child care worker Wanda Howell. She was holding two-year-old Dominique London, also dead, in her arms. Four infants had been resting in cribs located near the front of the building. They died at once. Four children outside the center also died. They had been visiting the federal building the day of the bombing.

Malissa McNeely recalled the moment she heard

about the bombing. She said, "I broke out in a frenzy, crying and shaking. I got the kids in the car and went downtown."[8] As a working mother, McNeely usually left her two children at the center. This was her day off and she had kept the children home. However, she knew that her sister's only child, Tony, was there. Tony died in the bombing.

Thu Nguyen and his wife were among those who waited fearfully at Children's Hospital. Their five-year-old son, Christopher, had been at the day care center. Now he was in surgery. An outraged Nguyen said, "I've seen war, O.K.? I've seen soldiers I fought with in Vietnam. . . . That was war. These are children. This is not a war. This is a crime."[9]

Many people wept when they saw a picture of firefighter Chris Fields holding the limp, bloodied body of Baylee Almon. Baylee had celebrated her first birthday the day before the bombing.

Baylee's grieving mother said, "I know my daughter is in heaven. I know she is."[10]

CHAPTER 3

Hope and Despair

Officials pledged to keep searching for any survivors. One woman standing near the site told reporters, "There's still hope. I've just been telling them to keep praying."[1]

As rescue teams pressed on, volunteers arrived. Donors lined up at Red Cross centers to give blood. Local restaurants supplied hamburgers, pizza, and other food to rescue crews, volunteers, and victims' families. People arrived with carloads of baby formula, flashlights, food, clothing, and other things. A sporting goods store in Stillwater, Oklahoma, shipped boxes of knee pads for the rescue workers.[2]

A team of sixty firefighters from Phoenix, Arizona, arrived soon after the bombing. They were experts at recovering bodies from rubble. By afternoon, it was clear that dozens of people were dead. Chief Phil Yeager of the Phoenix Fire Department told reporters:

> It's absolutely a race against time in slow motion. We have searched every area that you can just walk up to

and search. Now it's a matter of getting into those very dangerous, very unstable areas. . . . The possibility that there may be just one person in there is what keeps you going.[3]

In the fight to save lives, rescuers in hard hats used hydraulic saws to break up concrete. Cranes lifted large chunks of debris. Dogs sniffed the debris to locate bodies, dead or alive. One person found alive that first day was Priscilla Sayers. For nearly five terrifying hours, Sayers had lain buried, praying.

*S*earch and rescue teams dig through the rubble of what was once the Alfred P. Murrah Building.

Heavy winds arose, making rescue work harder. During the afternoon, workers were told to halt. Officials feared the building might collapse. But that evening, the struggle resumed. Giant spotlights were beamed onto the area.

A group of rescuers was thrilled to find twenty-year-old Daina Bradley. She was trapped in the basement. Her body lay beneath cement girders and a steel bar that was holding up heavy parts of the building. The firefighters knew they must use extreme care to remove the debris or tons of concrete could fall on her.

Dr. Gary Massad was one of the doctors who stayed with this victim among the debris. He watched nervously as Bradley's blood pressure dropped below normal. He later said, "My greatest fear was that I would be ordered to leave the building, that I would have to leave her trapped there."[4]

The men decided to cut the steel bar so they could reach Bradley. One of her legs was totally crushed. Doctors agreed they must cut it off below the knee to save her life. They faced another dilemma. Giving Bradley too much painkiller could send her into a coma. She endured horrible pain as doctors cut off her leg and freed her from the debris. Later, her rescuers learned that Bradley's mother and her two children had died in the bombing.

Was anyone else alive? As the night wore on, people began to lose hope. Among those who refused to give up were Dr. Rick Nelson and six colleagues. They had come as volunteers from a hospital in Muskogee, Oklahoma.

Dr. Gary Massad amputated twenty-year-old Daina Bradley's leg amid the rubble and debris, in order to save her life.

Suddenly, at about 10 P.M., Nelson heard someone shout, "We've got a live one!"[5]

A rescue dog had found a foot. It belonged to fifteen-year-old Brandy Liggons. Nelson said, "She was completely covered in rubble, twisted metal . . . of about two inches in diameter. She seemed to be wrapped around a metal chair."[6]

Slowly and carefully, workers removed the objects that trapped Liggons. They tried not to cause further injuries. Dr. Nelson held Liggons's hand and gave her oxygen. He talked and joked to keep up her spirits during the three-hour rescue. Finally, she was brought out and placed in an ambulance. During surgery, her injured spleen was removed. Liggons survived, despite bruised lungs and other injuries. Nelson said, "That girl's a miracle."[7]

While she was in the hospital, Brandy Liggons had a famous visitor: talk show host and actress Oprah Winfrey. Winfrey said she was inspired by Liggons's courage. She told her, "Brandy, if you can survive this, you can survive anything."[8]

Brandy Liggons was the last survivor found. All during the night and the next day, terrified families waited at the Red Cross and local churches. Had any other people been found? Tensely, people waited to find out.

Stephen Nix was among these anguished people. He waited all night for some word about his wife. At one point, he heard she was in a hospital. But that report turned out to be false. Nix said, "I get pumped up and then I get down. . . . And it's like a roller-coaster all day."[9] Thursday night, the family was still waiting.

In the days after the bombing, people brought dental records and descriptions of loved ones who were still missing. Dentists, fingerprint squads, and X-ray teams tried to match these up to the remains of bodies in the morgue.

Reverend Danny Cavett had an extremely painful job after the bombing. Cavett was the chaplain of Oklahoma City Children's Hospital. People were grieving over their losses and fearful about what would happen to their hospitalized loved ones. Cavett said, "It is their faces that I'll

A rescue dog like this one found fifteen-year-old Brandy Liggons alive among the rubble of the federal building.

*A*n unidentified family sits outside a Red Cross center, waiting for news about loved ones still missing, following the explosion.

never forget. So much frustration and fear. . . . It is the toughest thing I've ever been through."[10]

No other survivors had been found since the rescue of Brandy Liggons. Still, crews worked on for four days and nights. As Robert Billig prepared to go back Friday night, he said, "You look everywhere and you listen all the time and you hope."[11]

By now, people felt anger as well as grief. Investigations showed that the bomb had exploded from a van parked in front of the federal building. Investigators believed the bomb weighed around two tons. From the White House, President Clinton issued a

President Bill Clinton (shown at a memorial service with wife Hillary) called the people responsible for the bombing "evil cowards."

statement calling the persons responsible "evil cowards."[12]

On the day of the bombing, one bitter rescue crew painted these words on a brick wall at the bomb site:

We Search for the Truth.
We Seek Justice.
The Courts Require It.
The Victims Cry for It.
And GOD Demands It![13]

CHAPTER 4

"Find Out Who Did This"

Anger and bitterness spread as people witnessed the suffering caused by the bomb. President Clinton told people in Oklahoma City, "We pledge to do all we can to help you heal the injured, to rebuild this city, and to bring to justice those who did this evil."[1]

A firefighter told Oklahoma governor Frank Keating, "Find out who did this."[2]

Oliver (Buck) Revell, a former FBI assistant director, also spoke to the press. He said that this crime would most likely be solved. Revell said, "These people don't realize it, but they're going to leave a trail."[3]

People were now guessing who might have committed this crime. Some blamed foreign terrorists. Many thought that Middle Eastern terrorists were likely suspects. Some people of Arab descent reported being harassed or arrested for questioning. They feared they might be attacked or even killed.

Other people said an American militia group might be

to blame. Militias are nongovernmental, unofficial military groups that have expressed hatred and distrust toward the government. They oppose gun control laws. The Oklahoma bombing took place exactly two years after the 1993 siege at Waco, Texas. In Waco, federal agents had surrounded buildings where a religious group called Branch Davidians had gathered. The standoff between the Davidians and the agents lasted fifty-one days. On April 19, agents were told to enter the compound to remove illegal weapons and free anyone being held by force. Army helicopters and tanks arrived. Shots rang out, killing four federal agents. Fires quickly started and swept through the compound. Eighty-five Davidians died, including seventeen children. Militia groups blamed the fires and deaths on the government.

Some militias said the government might have bombed the federal building in order to pin the crime on their groups.

Others guessed that the bomber was a mentally unstable person with no political goal. Still other people wondered if a drug gang or other criminals had set off the bomb.

The FBI launched the biggest investigation in its history. Within an hour of the bombing, four teams of top agents went to the site. They brought special gear to gather and analyze evidence.

The FBI found important leads the day of the bombing. A cash machine video camera was operating nearby. The camera had recorded an image of a yellow Ryder van parked in front of the federal building just before the explosion.

One agent spotted a valuable clue two blocks from the federal building. It was a scrap of metal, part of a truck axle. The vehicle identification number (VIN) was still visible. The FBI traced this number and identified the vehicle as a 1993 Ford van. It came from a Ryder rental agency in Junction City, Kansas. Junction City was about 270 miles north of Oklahoma City.

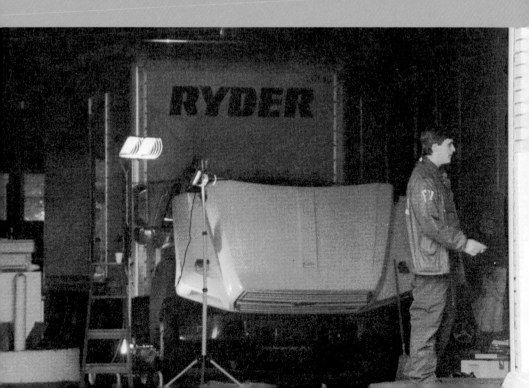

A Ryder van like this one was seen parked in front of the federal building just minutes before the explosion.

FBI agents were told that two men had rented this van on April 17. The men had used fake names and driver's licenses. Even so, FBI artists gained enough information to make sketches of the suspects. These suspects became known as John Doe No. 1 and John Doe No. 2. The suspects were both white American males. This terrorism had come from within, not from a foreign country. The FBI offered $2 million for information leading to a conviction.

A banner encourages rescue workers and shows the thanks of the people of Oklahoma City.

*F*lowers and teddy bears were placed on the fence surrounding the federal building as a silent memorial to those who died in the deadly blast.

Other agents combed the wreckage. Former FBI director James Fox said, "They are virtually touching every piece of brick and stone and dirt in that crater and putting it through a sifter."[4] They found crystals of ammonium nitrate on pieces of the rental van. It was mixed with fuel oil (racing-car fuel) to make a bomb.

While the FBI gathered evidence, rescue crews found more bodies in the rubble. After that first day, no one else was found alive. More than eight hundred people were being treated for injuries. The death count totaled 168, including nineteen children. Victims ranged in age from four months to seventy-three years old.

Nurse Rebecca Anderson was among the dead. She had been caring for victims when a piece of concrete struck her head. She died four days later. According to her wishes, her heart and kidneys were given to people awaiting organ transplants.

Oklahoma City was in pain. People came to stare at the bomb site. They placed flowers, ribbons, signs, and teddy bears on the chain-link fence that surrounded the area. Resident Mary Jennings said, "Everyone I know has a broken heart."[5]

Sunday was the fifth day after the bombing. A large community prayer service was held at the arena of the Oklahoma State Fairground.

Reverend Billy Graham addressed the mourners. He said, "That blast was like a violent explosion ripping at the heart of America. Long after the rubble is cleared and the rebuilding begins, the scars of this senseless and evil outrage will remain."[6]

CHAPTER 5

A Trail of Evidence

Within days of the bombing, the FBI announced they had a suspect in custody. The owner of a motel in Junction City recognized John Doe No. 1. He had stayed at the motel under the name Tim McVeigh.[1] He had signed in on April 14 and checked out on April 18—the day before the bombing.

A computer search revealed that a twenty-seven-year-old man named Timothy McVeigh was in jail in Perry, Oklahoma. McVeigh had been arrested the day of the bombing on unrelated charges. He had posted $500 bail and was scheduled for release in less than an hour.

At 10:20 A.M. on April 19, McVeigh's yellow Mercury Marquis had been stopped about sixty miles north of Oklahoma City. State trooper Charlie Hanger saw that the car had no license plate. He pulled McVeigh over. As the men were talking, Hanger saw a bulge under McVeigh's jacket. Reaching over, he discovered a semiautomatic pistol. McVeigh was also carrying a five-inch-long knife.

Hanger arrested McVeigh on concealed weapons charges. At that time, police did not connect him with the bombing. McVeigh spent two days at the county jail in Perry, Oklahoma.

The FBI later found a sealed envelope in the car McVeigh had driven on April 19. Inside were printed materials that criticized the United States government. Sections of some articles were highlighted. One passage discussed the killing of federal workers.

Officer Hanger also gave the FBI a business card McVeigh had left in his patrol car. It was from a military supply company in Wisconsin. On the back, these words had been written: "TNT at $5 a stick. Need more. Call after 01 May. See if you can get some more." McVeigh made no secret of his hatred toward the United States government.[2]

Formal charges were filed against McVeigh, and agents went to the Perry jail to take him to federal prison. As they left, angry crowds outside the jail yelled, "Baby-killer!"[3]

The FBI also located a man it thought might be John Doe No. 2. But six weeks after the bombing, he was cleared of suspicion. Rental shop records showed this man had come in a day later.[4]

By then, investigators had turned their attention to Terry Lynn Nichols. On his driver's license, McVeigh had given the address of Terry Nichols's brother James. McVeigh had served with Terry Nichols in the Persian Gulf War. Both men had ties to armed, antigovernment militias.

Reporters claimed that as many as one hundred thousand people throughout the nation belonged to militias.[5] These groups, often heavily armed, believe the government has too much control over people's lives. Some also say there is an international conspiracy to destroy or take over America.

With a warrant, FBI agents searched Terry Nichols's farm in Herington, Kansas. They found bomb-making materials and a receipt for ammonium nitrate. This substance had been used to make the Oklahoma City bomb.

Oklahoma City convicted bomber Timothy McVeigh had ties to an antigovernment militia.

Neighbors had seen a Ryder truck parked behind Nichols's home two days before the bombing.

In Nichols's basement, agents found blasting caps. They also found a drill bit that matched the marks left on a broken padlock at a nearby quarry. Explosives had been stolen from that quarry several months before the bombing. Inside Nichols's garage were white plastic barrels with blue lids—the same type used in the bombing.

Terry Nichols was arrested. FBI agents questioned him for nine hours. Investigators continued to gather clues.

Terry Nichols was charged with murder, conspiracy, and property destruction for his part in the bombing. All three charges carry the death penalty.

Timothy McVeigh and Terry Nichols were charged with murder, conspiracy, and destruction of government property. All three charges carry the death penalty.

Two seemingly ordinary men were charged with this horrible crime. Newsman Peter Jennings spoke to people who knew Timothy McVeigh. Jennings reported,

> Those who had known him most of his life all said the same thing—the Tim McVeigh they knew could not have done it. He was a nice kid, a smart boy. He was the creative one. He was happy. He was friendly."[6]

Yet the government said their case against him was solid.

A memorial service marked the one-year anniversary of the bombing. Some survivors left town that day because their memories were too painful. Thousands of others gathered at the site of the Alfred P. Murrah Federal Building. About six hundred firemen and rescue team members joined them. Many

A woman holds a rose and a program as she attends a memorial service to mark the one-year anniversary of the bombing.

grieving family members and survivors held roses. There were 168 seconds of silence in memory of those who died. The names of the victims were read.

After laying flowers on wreaths, people went to a public memorial service. Oklahoma governor Frank Keating said:

> At 9:02 on the morning of April 19th, 1995, we were together. We are together again today. Ours has been a very difficult journey. . . . I pray that each of us on this day of remembrance will look to our neighbors and remember that out of immense tragedy came an even greater outpouring of good.[7]

CHAPTER 6

Homegrown Terror

The trial of Timothy McVeigh started in the spring of 1997. It was held in Denver, Colorado, and was not televised. McVeigh had been raised in Upstate New York. During his junior year in high school, he began to collect guns. He also became interested in survivalism. McVeigh filled a cabinet with stored water and other things people need in an emergency.[1] After high school, he worked at a fast-food restaurant, then as an armored car guard.

During these months, McVeigh read a book called *The Turner Diaries*. Peter Jennings called the book "a violently racist novel about a band of white supremacists who foment a race war in order to overthrow the U.S. government."[2] Jennifer McVeigh said that her brother liked a passage on page 37. It said,

> With our original plan, we drive a truck into the main freight entrance of the FBI building and blow it up. We can wreak havoc in all the offices. Several hundred people will be killed.[3]

In May 1988, McVeigh joined the Army. Fellow soldiers recalled that McVeigh liked guns and gun magazines. During the Persian Gulf War, McVeigh earned a Bronze Star. He returned to his base at Fort Riley, Kansas. The Army was cutting jobs throughout 1991. It offered many people a voluntary discharge. McVeigh accepted.

Back home, McVeigh turned against the military. He read newspapers, journals, and magazines that criticized the government. Late in 1992, he left New York for Florida and became a gun dealer.

A jury had to decide if Timothy McVeigh should receive the death penalty for his role in the deaths of nineteen children in the bombing.

During 1993, McVeigh's former Army friend Terry Nichols joined him. McVeigh sometimes wrote angry letters to public officials, including President Clinton. He became enraged at the government again after the siege at Waco, Texas, in 1993.

That year, McVeigh moved to Arizona. He renewed his friendship with another Army friend, Michael Fortier. Fortier would later say that McVeigh tested at least one ammonium nitrate fertilizer bomb in 1994.

At McVeigh's trial, Fortier testified against McVeigh. He said that he had watched McVeigh plan the bombing. On October 20, 1993, the two men allegedly went to Oklahoma City so McVeigh could check out the federal building. Fortier said that he and Terry Nichols went along when McVeigh viewed the building again in 1994.

There was important testimony regarding the Ryder truck and the getaway car. Fortier said that McVeigh had told him where he planned to park his getaway car. This turned out to be the place where FBI agents had found a key lying on the ground. The key belonged to the Ryder rental truck that had carried the bomb.

Michael Fortier's wife, Lori, also took the stand. According to Lori Fortier, "Tim told us he wanted to blow up a building, a federal building." McVeigh had told her that the Oklahoma federal building was a good choice, because it was an easy target with a glass front.[4]

Other witnesses said that Nichols and McVeigh had bought several fifty-pound bags of ammonium nitrate fertilizer in two towns in Kansas. One of McVeigh's fingerprints was on the receipt from the purchase in McPherson, Kansas. Other witnesses said McVeigh and Nichols had bought $2,850 worth of racing fuel at a Texas racetrack.

The defense then presented its case. Defense Attorney Stephen Jones tried to discredit prosecution witnesses. He told the jury that they could not rely on test results from the FBI lab. McVeigh did not testify in his own defense.

*T*his American flag at the federal building was a reminder that Americans were no longer safe from terrorism in their own country.

The jury of seven men and five women deliberated for three days. They reached a unanimous verdict: guilty.

The jury next had to decide whether to enforce the death penalty. Assistant U.S. Attorney Beth Wilkinson gave the closing statement for the prosecution. She said,

> Take a moment and look at Timothy McVeigh. Look into the eyes of a coward, and tell him you will have the courage. Tell him you will speak with one unified voice, as the moral conscience of the community, and tell him he is no patriot. He is a traitor, and he deserves to die."[5]

Again, the jurors reached a unanimous decision. McVeigh was sentenced to death.

He was executed by lethal injection on June 11, 2001. McVeigh was the first federal prisoner to be executed in thirty-eight years. The trial of Terry Nichols began on September 29, 1997—a little over three months after Timothy McVeigh was sentenced to death. Nichols was sentenced to life in prison for his part in the bombing.

Studies show that militia groups increased in number after the April 19 bombing. In October 1994, the Anti-Defamation League (ADL) issued a report called "Armed and Dangerous: Militias Take Aim at the Federal Government." They found militia groups in thirteen states with about ten thousand members.[6]

A follow-up report in 1995 showed militia groups in forty states. These groups claimed about fifteen thousand members.[7] Some militias were using the Internet to recruit members. They included white supremacy groups, such as White Aryans and neo-Nazis.

Many experts agree that Americans can no longer feel safe from acts of terrorism. Some would like the government to completely ban unofficial military groups.

Meanwhile, the victims of the Oklahoma City bombing have not been forgotten. A chain-link fence surrounds the grass-covered lot where the building once stood. On the fence, people place photos of the victims and handwritten notes. Tourists come to pray.

Life has changed for the survivors. After the bombing, Michael Reyes said his co-workers became closer. He said,

We check up on each other every day. Everybody checks up on everybody, at least in our own little areas, and we know who's not doing well, and you can't help being close knit.[8]

Reyes said that some survivors remained fearful: "Some people equate work with death, and you're not supposed to equate work with death."[9]

Over time, most of the federal employees who survived have been able to return to work. There are a number who are still struggling emotionally from the aftershocks of the blast.[10]

Victims of the bombing will never be forgotten. Rescue workers stand for a moment of silence as they recall the lives lost in the tragic blast.

Government buildings have hired more guards and have banned parking nearby. Local police forces have met with federal law enforcement agents to discuss ways to prevent and deal with terrorism.

Joe Hansen was the assistant fire chief in Oklahoma City. He called it "a humbling experience." But he said, "I am proud of how everybody pulled together and kind of bonded in this. This sends a signal to the terrorists . . . that they may wound us but they will never defeat us."[11]

Other Related Disasters

DATE	DESCRIPTION
September 5, 1972	Arab terrorists shoot and kill eleven members of the Israeli Olympic team at the Summer Olympic Games in Munich, Germany.
October 23, 1983	Shiite Muslim suicide bomber kills 241 servicemen in Beirut, Lebanon.
October 7, 1985	Four members of the Palestinian Liberation Organization take over the Italian cruise ship *Achille Lauro* in open seas near Port Said, Egypt. One passenger, an American man, is shot and killed before the hijackers surrender on October 9, 1985.
December 1988	Pan Am Flight 103 is bombed over Lockerbie, Scotland, by Libyan terrorists. Two hundred seventy people are killed.
September 1989	UTA Flight 772 is bombed over Niger by Libyan terrorists. One hundred seventy-one people are killed.
April 10, 1992	Irish Republican Army (IRA) claims responsibility for a car bomb that explodes in the London financial district. Three people are killed; ninety-one are injured.
March 20, 1995	Japanese terrorists release sarin, a poisonous nerve gas, in five Tokyo subway cars. Twelve people are killed; fifty-five hundred are injured. Members of the religious cult Aum Shinrikyo later claim responsibility.
April 19, 1995	Japanese terrorists release phosgene, a poisonous gas, in a crowded train in Yokahama, Japan.
April 19, 1995	Alfred P. Murrah Federal Building in Oklahoma City is bombed. One hundred sixty-eight people are killed; hundreds are injured.
July 25, 1995	A bomb explodes in a crowded commuter train in Paris, France. Four people die instantly; eight others are injured, some critically.
November 13, 1995	U.S. Air Force Base military training and communications center in Riyadh, Saudi Arabia, is bombed. Six people are killed.
February 25, 1996	Hamas, a Palestinian terrorist group, bombs an Israeli bus in West Jerusalem. Twenty-four passengers and the bomber are killed.
April 18, 1996	Islamic militants shoot and kill eighteen Greek tourists outside a hotel in Cairo, Egypt.

Chapter Notes

Chapter 1. "This Isn't Supposed to Happen"

1. Bill Hewitt and Bob Stewart, "April Mourning," *People*, May 15, 1995, p. 101.

2. "Survivors of Oklahoma City Bombing Recall the Day," National Public Radio, *Morning Edition* with Bob Edwards, April 19, 1996.

3. Ibid.

4. Quoted in Richard A. Serrano, "April 19, 1995," *Los Angeles Times Magazine*, Sunday April 13, 1997, p. 16.

5. Ibid.

6. "No Place to Hide," *48 Hours*, CBS News, April 20, 1995, Burelle's Transcripts, p. 3.

7. Quoted in Serrano, p. 14.

Chapter 2. Hours of Agony

1. Nancy Gibbs et al., "The Blood of Innocents," *Time*, May 1, 1995, p. 59.

2. Ibid.

3. Ibid.

4. Ibid., p. 62.

5. "Survivors of Oklahoma City Bombing Recall the Day," *Morning Edition*, National Public Radio with Bob Edwards, April 19, 1996.

6. Bob Stewart, "Answers to a Prayer," *People*, May 15, 1995, p. 106.

7. Testimony from the penalty phase of the trial of Timothy McVeigh, quoted in Tom Morganthau and Peter Annin, "Should McVeigh Die?" *Newsweek*, June 16, 1997, p. 22.

8. Linda Kramer, "A Sister's Luck, Another's Loss," *People*, May 15, 1995, pp. 101–102.

9. Gibbs et al., p. 62.

10. Ibid., p. 64.

Chapter 3. Hope and Despair

1. "No Place to Hide," *48 Hours*, CBS News, April 20, 1995, Burelle's Transcripts, p. 9.

2. Nancy Gibbs et al., "The Blood of Innocents," *Time*, May 1, 1995, p. 64.

3. "No Place to Hide," p. 9.

4. Gibbs et al., p. 61.

5. Gail Wescott, "The Last Life Saved," *People*, May 15, 1995, p. 104.

6. Gibbs et al., p. 63.

7. Ibid.

8. "The 8-Minute Key to Happiness: Celebrity Inspiration," *Woman's World*, March 5, 1997, p. 9.

9. "No Place to Hide," p. 11.

10. Carlton Stowers, "Healing Spirit," *People*, May 15, 1995, p. 103.

11. John Leland, Debra Rosenberg, and Karen Springen, "I Think About It All the Time," *Newsweek*, May 8, 1995, p. 35.

12. Evan Thomas et al., "Cleverness—and Luck," *Newsweek*, May 1, 1995, p. 30; James Carney, "Measure of a President," *Time*, May 1, 1997, p. 65.

13. Richard A. Serrano, "Two Years Ago, a Bomb Ripped Through the Alfred P. Murrah Federal Building in Oklahoma City," *Los Angeles Times Magazine*, April 13, 1997, p. 16.

Chapter 4. "Find Out Who Did This"

1. James Carney, "Measure of a President," *Time*, May 1, 1995, p. 65.

2. Nancy Gibbs et al., "The Blood of Innocents," *Time*, May 1, 1995, p. 57.

3. Evan Thomas et al., "Cleverness—and Luck," *Newsweek*, May 1, 1995, p. 31.

4. "No Place to Hide," *48 Hours*, CBS News, April 20, 1995, Burrelle's Transcripts, p. 20.

5. Evan Thomas et al., "The Plot," *Newsweek*, May 8, 1995, p. 34.

6. Quoted in Richard A. Serrano, "April 15, 1995," *Los Angeles Times Magazine*, April 13, 1997, p. 14.

Chapter 5. A Trail of Evidence

1. Evan Thomas et al., "Cleverness—and Luck," *Newsweek*, May 1, 1995, p. 34.

2. Richard A. Serrano, "Trooper Testifies on McVeigh's Arrest," *Los Angeles Times*, April 29, 1997, p. A-20.

3. Thomas et al., p. 35.

4. "John Doe Number Two," *Good Morning America*, ABC, May 6, 1997.

5. Tom Morganthau et al., "The View From the Far Right," *Newsweek*, May 1, 1995, p. 36.

6. *ABC News* Special Report: "Peter Jennings Reporting: Who Is Tim McVeigh?" ABC News, 1997.

7. "Voices in the News Last Week," Sunday, *Weekend Edition* with Liane Hanson, National Public Radio, April 21, 1996.

Chapter 6. Homegrown Terror

1. *ABC News* Special Report: "Peter Jennings Reporting: Who Is Tim McVeigh?" ABC News, 1997.

2. Ibid.

3. Ibid.

4. Ibid.

5. Peter Annin and Tom Morganthau, "The Verdict: Death," *Newsweek*, June 23, 1997, p. 41.

6. Anti-Defamation League, "Armed and Dangerous: Militias Take Aim at the Federal Government," New York: ADL, 1994, p. 1.

7. Anti-Defamation League, "Beyond the Bombing: The Militia Menace Grows," New York: ADL, 1995, p. 1.

8. "Survivors of Oklahoma City Bombing Recall the Day," National Public Radio, *Morning Edition* with Bob Edwards, April 19, 1996.

9. Ibid.

10. Ibid.

11. Quoted in Associated Press Wire Services, "Oklahoma City Honors Blast Victims," *Los Angeles Times*, April 20, 1997, p. A-18.

blood bank—A center for collecting and giving out blood needed by accident victims and others, such as surgical patients.

militia group—Unofficial, armed military groups whose members express hatred and distrust toward the government.

terrorism—The use of violence to frighten, hurt, and kill people in order to gain or maintain political power.

terrorist—A person who uses violence, either toward specific targets or randomly, to achieve political goals.

white supremacy groups—Groups whose members believe that white people are superior to other races. They believe white people should dominate those other races.

Further Reading

Books

Able, Deborah. *Hate Groups.* Hillside, N.J.: Enslow Publishers, Inc., 1995.

Davis, Lee. *Man-Made Catastrophes.* New York: Facts on File, 1993.

Hyde, Margaret O., and Elizabeth H. Forsyth. *Terrorism: A Special Kind of Violence.* New York: Dodd, Mead, 1987.

Kronenwetter, Michael. *United They Hate: White Supremacist Groups in America.* New York: Walker, 1992.

Landau, Elaine. *Terrorism: America's Growing Threat.* New York: Dutton Lodestar, 1992.

———. *White Power Movement: America's Racist Hate Groups.* Brookfield, Conn.: The Millbrook Press, 1993.

Lang, Susan S. *Extremist Groups in America.* New York: Franklin Watts, 1990.

Raynor, Thomas P. *Terrorism: Past, Present, and Future.* New York: Franklin Watts, 1982.

Internet Sites

<http://www.fema.gov/okc95/index.htm>

<http://www.cnn.com/US/OKC/memorial/index.html>

<http://www.oklahoman.net/connections/memorial>